T0008083

For Tom, who has always loved looking in ponds

JP

Love and thanks to my toadally awesome family!

NC

First US edition 2023

Library of Congress Catalog Card Number 2022907271
ISBN 978-1-5362-2513-6

23 24 25 26 27 28 APS 10 9 8 7 6 5 4 3 2 1

Printed in Humen, Dongguan, China

This book was typeset in Nevis Bold and Zalderdash.
The illustrations were created digitally.

Candlewick Press
99 Dover Street
Somerville, Massachusetts 02144

www.candlewick.com

So You Want to Be a

JANE PORTER illustrated by NEIL CLARK

Welcome to Frog Club.

So you want to be a frog?
Of course you do. Who wouldn't?
But do you have what it *really* takes?

I'm Fabio Frog—yes, it does sound
a bit like "fabulous"—and I'm
going to be your coach today.

Stretch those legs!
You're going to need some
very special skills.

FROG CLUB CHECKLIST

CAN YOU:

sit still for hours?

catch food with just your tongue?

thrive on flies?

stare without blinking?

breathe underwater?

hop twenty times your body length?

drink through your skin?

Not so simple, is it?

But come on, why don't you give it a try?

Before we begin . . .

Let's take a look at you! Hmm.
You're not exactly green, are you?

Still, we frogs do sometimes come in other colors. You should see my cousin the Malagasy Rainbow Frog and my friend the Glass Frog, who has transparent skin. You can even see her heart beating! So maybe there's *some* hope for you.

Just look at them!

How do you feel about getting wet?
We frogs belong to a very exclusive group: the AMPHIBIANS.
That means we live part of our life in the water and part on land—and we can breathe through both our skin *and* our lungs.
Impressive, aren't we?

Here at Frog Club, we have a secret saying:
Stay damp! Stay shady! Stay cool! Don't forget it!
Now it's time for you to learn our Frog Club rules.
I think I hear a splash. Let's head for the pond!

RULE ONE: Start small and wriggle well

Believe it or not, I wasn't always this good-looking. I started life as a teeny, tiny dot in a big blob of frog eggs.

Then I grew into a little curl inside that blob of jelly.

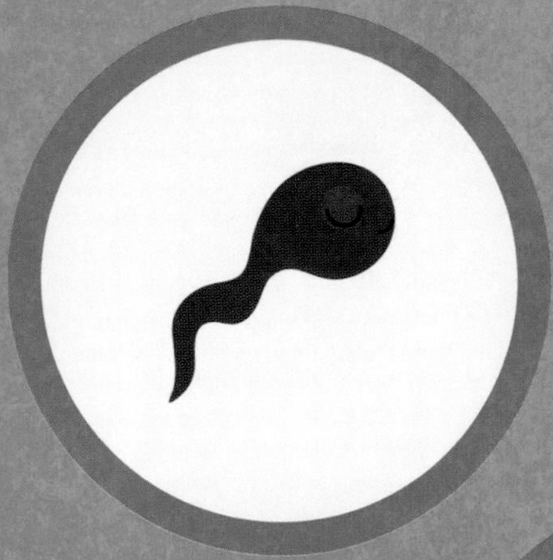

After that, I started wriggling . . . and before I knew it, I was a tadpole.

After all that wriggling, I grew legs, then arms, and then my tail disappeared. I was a tiny frog at last.

Let's see how small you can go . . .
Curl yourself up—really tiny.
Now, are you any good at
wriggling? Give it a try!
Hmm, I know you can wriggle
faster than that. Keep going!
Looking good!

Now follow my
tadpole friends to
the next page . . .

RULE TWO: Jump far, jump often

You know what's great about my legs? They let me jump a REALLY long way. How far can you jump? Go on, give it a try. Hmm. That's not very good, is it?

If a frog were as big as you, it would be able to leap the length of two buses.

Stick your tongue out and see
how far it can go.
Oh dear, is that all?

RULE THREE: Choose your colors carefully

To be a frog like me, you need to be handsome, smooth, wet, clever . . . and most importantly, GREEN.

Ahh, was there ever a better color? Which is your favorite green?

Emerald Glass Frog

*Hey!
What's that? Are you saying we're not all green?*

Bird-Voiced Tree Frog

White-Lipped Tree Frog

*Aha—well remembered!
You're pretty smart for a human.*

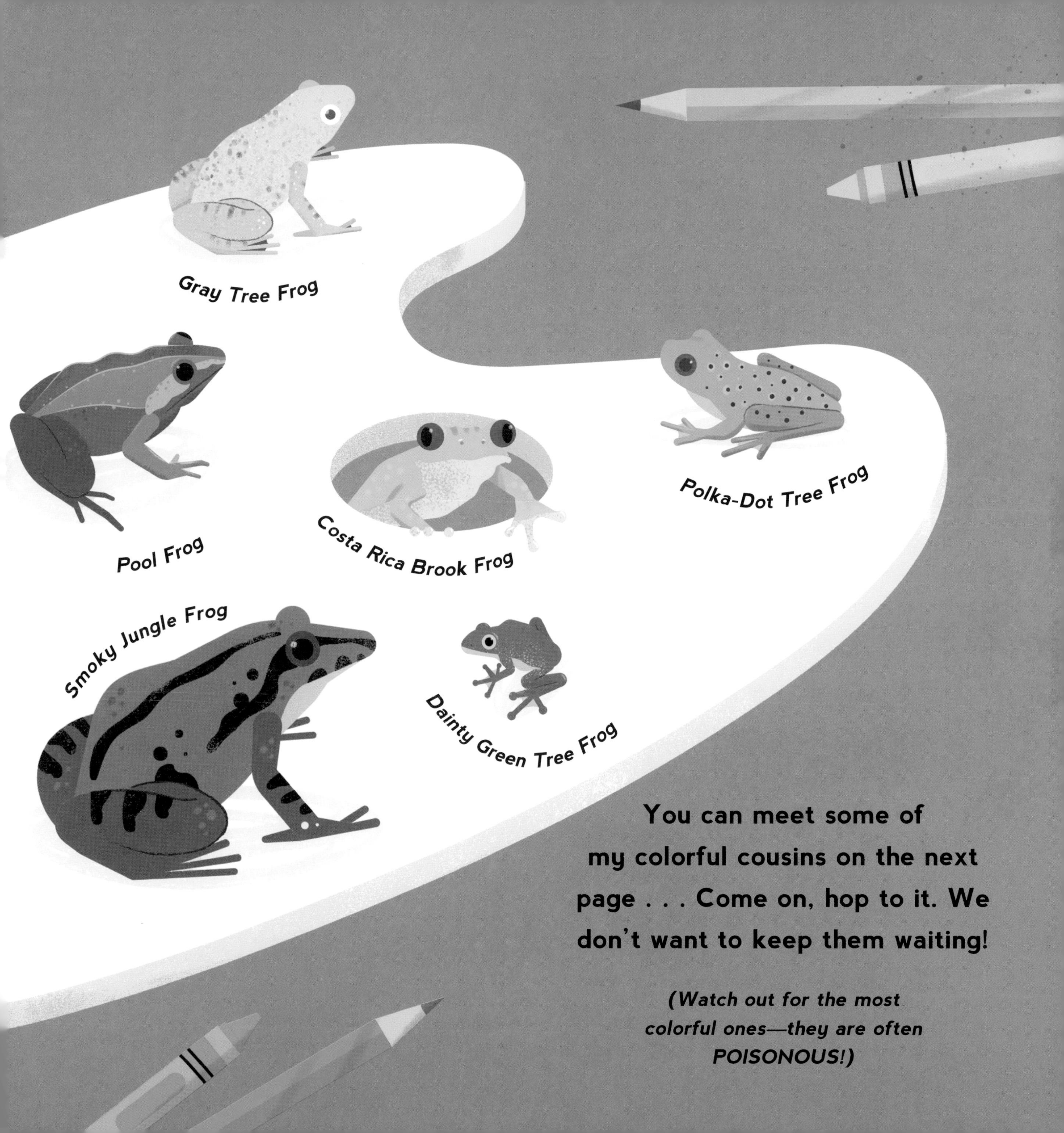

You can meet some of my colorful cousins on the next page . . . Come on, hop to it. We don't want to keep them waiting!

(Watch out for the most colorful ones—they are often POISONOUS!)

RULE FOUR: Make friends around the world

Here are just a few of my froggy friends and relatives. Can you guess how many different types of us there are all over the world?

Nearly FIVE THOUSAND!

You can find us on every continent of the world, except Antarctica.

We don't all live in ponds. My cousins the tree frogs live high up in tropical branches, where their special toe pads help them hang on tight.

How's it hanging?

There are even a few of us who live in deserts! The Desert Rain Frog burrows underground to escape the hot sun during dry months.

In Alaska, Wood Frogs freeze themselves during the winter, then hop away when spring comes.

RULE FIVE: Have a froggy hero

Big frogs, tiny frogs, hairy frogs, flying frogs . . . What sort of frog do YOU want to be?

Meet the biggest frog in the world—it's as heavy as a rabbit. And a BIG rabbit at that!

Goliath Frog

Ornate Horned Frog

Imagine your mouth was half the size of your whole body! No wonder its nickname is the Pacman Frog.

Golden Dart Frog

Careful! This is one of the most poisonous animals on earth. One tiny frog has enough toxin to kill TWO elephants.

Wallace's Flying Frog

This frog glides through the air as if it can really FLY! Can you? Stretch your arms right out and imagine you've got wings between your fingers.

Ah! I see you have hair, like most humans! Don't worry—you won't need to cut it off to be a frog. Some of us are actually hairy, like my fuzzy friend here. The hairs help him breathe underwater.

Hairy Frog

Look out! Here's the smallest frog in the world—it's as tiny as a fly. It's got a very big name, though!

Paedophryne amauensis

RULE SIX: Connect with your ancient ancestors

How old are you, anyway? I don't mean YOU—I mean humans! We frogs have been on earth for more than two hundred million years, but people have been around for only about two million years. Babies!

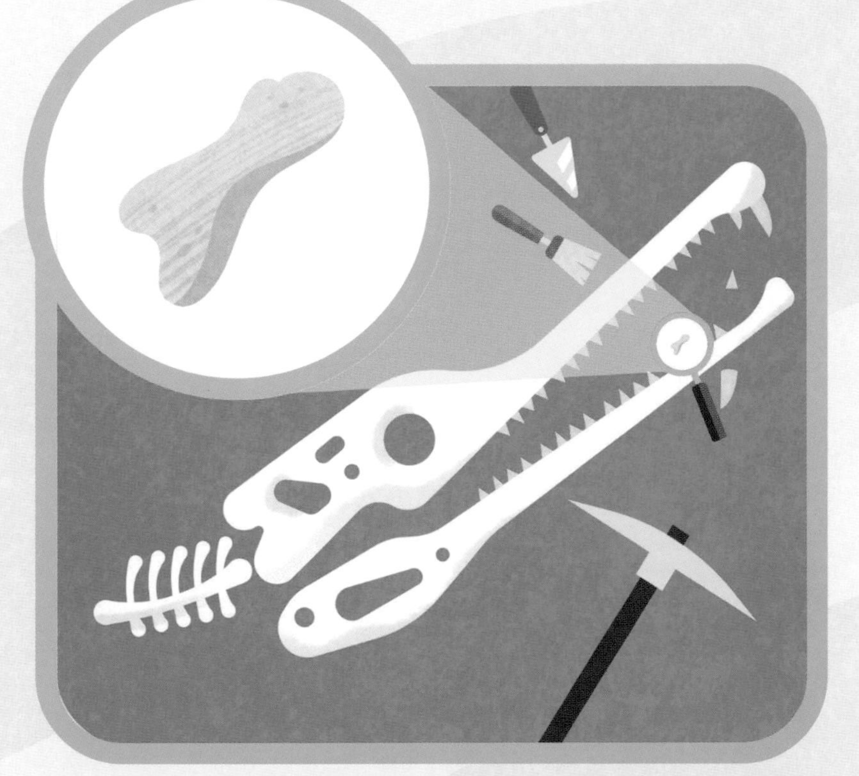

In Arizona, scientists found a tiny bit of bone among some giant crocodile skeletons. That bone turned out to be from one of my relatives, which lived about 216 million years ago.

In Myanmar, they discovered a piece of amber with a tiny frog inside—from 99 million years ago. This now-extinct frog has an exciting name: *Electrorana*.

And over in Madagascar, they found fossilized remains of my distantly related great-uncle *Beelzebufo*, from 68 million years ago.

He was as big as a beach ball and could eat baby dinosaurs with his great strong jaws.

Do you think YOU would enjoy eating a baby dinosaur? No, I didn't think so.

RULE SEVEN: Choose flies for flavor

For me, the perfect dinner is a fresh, live fly. Frogs would rather starve than eat anything that's already dead. Ugh!

Take a look at the Frog Club menu. I've added some treats for you and some for me, so choose carefully!

Hint: if you're not tempted by slugs or flies, maybe you're not ready to be a frog just yet.

We frogs use our eyes to swallow food—when we blink, our eyeballs help push the food down our throats.

Can you blink and swallow at the same time?

RULE EIGHT: Make some noise!
You've been a bit quiet. Time to try some croaking. Some of us frogs can chirp, grunt, and even whistle!
Ribbit! Ribbit!
Western Chorus Frog
Preeeee preeeeeee preeeee
Peep-peep peep-peep
Pripppipprippipp
Spring Peeper Frog
Mink Frog

Rrr-rrr-rumm!

Rrrr-rumm!

Bullfrog

Wood Frog

Cluck-cluck
cluck-cluck

Chickachickachicka

Northern Cricket Frog

Now it's your turn.
Say it with me:

croak,
CROAK, CROAK!

Louder! Some frogs can be heard over a mile away.

Beautiful! You're getting good at this. Were you born in a pond by any chance?

RULE NINE: Know how to be more frog

We love to hang out together. Did you know a group of frogs is called an army? Sometimes it's also called a knot or a colony.

Here's another funny thing about frogs: we shed our skin about once a week . . . and then we eat it. Tasty!

Some frogs hibernate, which means we go to sleep for the winter. While we do, our bones grow a new ring, just like a tree trunk does.

Being more frog means keeping safe, too. Cats, herons, and foxes ALL love to snack on us—so we keep really, really still to make sure they don't spot us.

Watch out! There's a cat coming now! Can you keep still—I mean REALLY still?

Oh dear, I saw you twitch. Try again.
Yes! That's a bit better.
I suppose we might make a frog of you yet.

RULE TEN: Keep cool in the pool

Now that we're friends, would you like to come over to my place? Better put your rain boots on. I know you humans don't like getting wet feet. Strange!

Make yourself comfortable on that lily pad. Be careful—don't fall off. Let me show you around my pond.

We can breathe underwater through our skin, AND we can drink water through it, too. We have a special "drinking patch" on our tummies and thighs.

See these reeds? We love to sit among them, hidden away from the sun. That's because we frogs are cold-blooded. If the sun is hot, we get hot—so we love a shady spot.

I like to stay cool by sitting in the water with only my eyes showing. I can go for a long time without blinking. Want to try?

I bet I can beat you!

You've done well! Your croaking, wriggling, and jumping are top-notch—but you need a bit more practice staying still.